I0759899

MORE THE ART OF MIXOLOGY™ TITLES

The Art of Mixology

The Bartender's Guide to Bourbon and Whiskey

The Bartender's Guide to Gin

The Bartender's Guide to Rum

The Essential Guide to Cocktails

Mean Girls Totally Fetch Mocktails

Mocktails

Making Spirits Bright

Activity Books and Sets

The Art of Mixology Word Search: Intoxicating Puzzles

Sips & Snacks Recipe Card Box Set

Cocktail Recipe Card Box Set

Wine Trivia Card Box Set

Cozy Cocktails

5005 Newport Drive, Rolling Meadows, Illinois 60008

Cover illustrated by Gareth Williams
Photography by Mike Cooper, Günter Beer, and Powell Jordano
Additional photos used under license from Shutterstock.com

ISBN 979-8-89019-163-2

Notes for the Reader

Unless otherwise indicated, this book uses standard kitchen measuring spoons and cups. All spoon and cup measurements are level. Milk is assumed to be whole, eggs are large, individual vegetables are medium, and pepper is freshly ground black pepper. All root vegetables should be peeled prior to using. People with nut allergies should be aware that some of the prepared ingredients used in the recipes in this book may contain nuts.

Garnishes, decorations, and serving suggestions are all optional and not necessarily included in the recipe ingredients or method. The times given are only an approximate guide. Preparation times differ according to the techniques used by different people and the cooking times may also vary from those given. Optional ingredients, variations, or serving suggestions have not been included in the time calculations.

Please consume alcohol responsibly.

Cozy Cocktails

PARRAGON™

CONTENTS

INTRODUCTION

There's a reason fall is many people's favorite time of year. The bitter cold of winter hasn't yet arrived, but there's a brisk nip in the air, perfect for comfortably cozying up in a soft sweater or under a favorite blanket. And fall activities draw generations of family and friends to spend much-loved quality time together. There's no denying that a good cocktail is the perfect complement to a delicious meal among loved ones, time spent around a bonfire, or after a day at a pumpkin patch or farm. In this book, you'll find a collection of cozy cocktails perfect for fall and any festive activity.

You can enjoy carving pumpkins with a complementary Pumpkin Spice Moscow Mule (page 43) or a Pumpkin Old Fashioned (page 48) in hand. Warm up with a Bourbon Apple Cider (page 81) or a mug of Spiked Cinnamon Tea (page 97) after spending a brisk day apple picking or taking little ones trick-or-treating on a chilly night. And hosting a Halloween party will be extra spooky if you're serving a bowl of Phantom Punch (page 66) or a Witch-tini (page 58). It's also worth noting that many of the recipes included in this book can easily be made as a mocktail for children or for adults who prefer their drinks sans alcohol. These drinks are sure to make everyone's fall season warm and cozy.

GLASSWARE

Presentation is everything in mixology, so it is important to serve a cocktail in the appropriate glass—the size, shape, and style all have an impact on the visual perception and enjoyment of the drink. Here are some of the classic glasses you will need to have in your collection.

Martini Glass

The most iconic of all cocktail glasses, the conical glass emerged with the art deco movement. The long stem is perfect for chilled drinks, because it keeps people's hands from inadvertently warming the cocktail.

Highball Glass

Sometimes known as a Collins glass, these glasses are perfect for serving drinks with a high proportion of mixer to alcohol. The highball glass is versatile enough to be a substitute for the similarly shaped, but slightly larger, Collins glass.

Old-Fashioned Glass

The lowball glass, also known as a rocks glass, is a short, squat tumbler and is great for serving any alcohol on the rocks, or for short, mixed cocktails.

Champagne Flute

The tall, thin flute's tapered design reduces the champagne's surface area and so helps to keep the fizz in the drink for longer. The flute has now largely replaced the coupe glass for serving champagne and champagne cocktails.

Shot Glass

This glass is a home bar essential and can hold just enough alcohol to be drunk in one mouthful. It also has a firm base that can be satisfyingly slammed on a bar top. The shot glass can also stand in for a measure when making cocktails.

Margarita Glass

The margarita, or coupette, glass, as its name implies, was designed specifically for serving margaritas. It is ideal for any frozen, blended drinks.

Coupe Glass

A wide-rim glass that is good for serving sparkling drinks was once the glass of choice for champagne. Legend has it that the glass was inspired by the shape of a woman's breast.

Snifter Glass

The bowl-shape snifter glass invites drinkers to cradle the drink in their hands, warming the contents of the glass—it is good for winter liquors, such as brandy. The aroma of the drink is held in the glass, allowing you to breathe in the drink before sipping.

Hurricane Glass

This pear-shaped glass pays homage to the hurricane lamp and was used to create the New Orleans rum-based cocktail: the Hurricane. It's also used for a variety of frozen and blended cocktails.

Iced Beverage Glass

A variation on the highball glass that combines a tapered, tall bowl with a short stem, this glass is ideal for serving chilled drinks.

Irish Coffee Glass

The mug of this type of glass typically sits on top of a decorative pedestal foot. Its handle makes it an elegant and safe way to enjoy hot beverages.

MIXOLOGY EQUIPMENT

The equipment you have in your home bar depends on whether you are a cocktail king or queen who likes all the latest gadgets, or whether you are prepared to make do with some basic options. Nowadays, there is no limit to the amount of bar equipment available, but you definitely won't need a lot of gimmicky gadgets to make the majority of the drinks in this book. Here is an outline of the essential tools of the trade.

Jigger

A jigger is a bartender's basic measuring tool and is essential for crafting the perfect blend of ingredients. It usually has a measurement on each end, such as 1 ounce and 1½ ounces. Look for a steel jigger with clear measurement markings so you can easily and accurately pour out the measures.

Barspoon

A proper barspoon has a small bowl and a long handle that allows you to muddle, mix, and stir with ease. Spoons come in a variety of lengths and widths, and a stylish barspoon is an attractive addition to any bartender's equipment.

Shaker

Most contemporary shakers are made from steel, because steel doesn't tarnish readily and doesn't conduct heat easily—this is useful for chilled cocktails, because the ice cools the cocktail instead of the shaker. Most standard shakers come with a built-in strainer, but if you're using a Boston or Parisian shaker, you'll need to use a separate strainer.

Mixing Glass

Any vessel that holds about 2 cups of liquid can be used for mixing drinks. It is good to have a mixing glass with a spout or ridged rim so that you can stop ice from slipping into the glass; however, this is not vital, because you can always use a strainer. Mixing glasses are increasingly popular, and they are usually made of glass or crystal.

Muddler

For mashing up citrus fruit or crushing herbs, you need a muddler. This is a chunky wooden tool with a rounded end, and it can also be used to make cracked ice. You can mash fruit or crush herbs with a mortar and pestle, but the advantage of a muddler is that it can be used directly in the mixing glass.

Strainer

A bar or Hawthorne strainer is an essential tool to prevent ice and other ingredients from being poured into your glass. Some cocktails need to be double strained, so even if there is a strainer in your cocktail shaker, you'll still need a separate Hawthorne strainer in your bar collection.

Juicer

A traditional juicer, with a ridged half-lemon shape on a saucer, works well for juicing small amounts. There is also a citrus spout available that screws into a lemon or lime; it is useful for obtaining tiny amounts of juice. Mechanical or electric presses are great for large amounts of juice, but they are not essential in a home bar.

Other Equipment

Other items you might need in your home bar equipment are a corkscrew, bottle opener, decorative toothpicks, blender, tongs, ice bucket, cutting board, knives, pitchers, swizzle sticks, straws, and an espuma gun for making foams.

MIXOLOGY TECHNIQUES

Shaking and Stirring

These are the two most basic mixology techniques, and they are essential to master to confidently make a range of classic and craft cocktails. Shaking is when you add all the ingredients, with the specified amount of ice cubes, to the shaker and shake vigorously for 5–10 seconds. The benefits of shaking are that the drink is rapidly mixed, chilled, and aerated. Once the drink has been shaken, the outside of the shaker should be lightly frosted. Shaking a cocktail will dilute your drink significantly. This is an essential part of the cocktail-making process and gives recipes the correct balance of taste, strength, and temperature. After shaking, the drink is double strained into glasses—the shaker should have a built-in strainer, but you may also use a separate strainer over the glass. Shaking can also be used to prepare cocktails that include an ingredient that will not combine with less vigorous forms of mixing, such as an egg white.

Stirring is the purist's choice. This is a mixing technique where you add all the ingredients, usually with some ice cubes, but you combine them in a mixing glass and then stir the ingredients together using a long-handled barspoon or swizzle stick. This allows for you to blend and chill the ingredients without too much erosion of the ice, so you can control the level of dilution and keep it to a minimum.

Building and Layering

Building is a technique of pouring all the ingredients, one by one, usually over ice into the serving glass. You might then stir the cocktail briefly, but this is just to mix instead of to chill or aerate. The order the ingredients are added can change from drink to drink, which can affect the final flavor.

Another important bartending skill is the art of layering, requiring concentration, precision, and a steady hand. To make layered drinks, you generally pour the heaviest liquid first, working to the lightest. The real trick is the technique. Touch the top of the drink with a long-handled barspoon and pour the liquid slowly over the back of it to disperse it across the top of the ingredients already in the glass. Be sure to use a clean barspoon for each layer. Floating is the term used to describe adding the top layer.

Muddling and Blending

Muddling is the extraction of the juice or oils from the pulp or skin of a fruit, herb, or spice and involves mashing ingredients to release their flavors. It's usually done with a wooden pestle-like implement called a muddler. (If you don't have a muddler, use a mortar and pestle or the end of a wooden spoon.) The best muddling technique is to keep pressing down with a twisting action until the ingredient has released all its oil or juice.

Blending is when all the cocktail ingredients are combined in a blender or food processor. This technique is often used when mixing alcohol with fruit or with creamy ingredients that do not combine well otherwise. Use crushed or cracked ice to produce cocktails with a smooth, frozen consistency.

Foams

Foams and airs can be created in various thicknesses, from a light froth to a heavy, creamy foam. For a simple foam, use egg white, lemon juice, and sugar. To top 2 cocktails, whisk 1 egg white with ½ ounce of lemon juice and 1 teaspoon of granulated sugar until thoroughly mixed. Put the mixture into an espuma gun or cream whipper, then charge, shake, and spray it over the top of the cocktails for a light, creamy finish. The fresher the egg white, the more stable the foam, so use fresh eggs.

CHAPTER ONE

Leaves are falling and apples are ready to be picked. With ingredients like hard apple cider to apple brandy, in this section you'll find cocktails where the star fall flavor is apples.

AUTUMN APPLE

SERVES 6

juice of 3 small oranges
5 ounces Calvados or other apple brandy
few dashes vanilla extract
3 cups hard apple cider, chilled
apple slices, to garnish

1. Mix the first four ingredients in a pitcher, then add ice.
2. Pour mixture into each glass and garnish with a slice of apple.

THE APPLE TEASER

SERVES 8

⅓ ounce whiskey
⅓ ounce amaretto
⅓ ounce Calvados
1 dash grenadine
¾ ounce apple juice
club soda, for topping
apple slice, to garnish

1. In a cocktail shaker filled with ice, combine the first five ingredients. Shake until well frosted.
2. Strain into a highball glass filled with ice and top off with club soda to taste. Garnish with a slice of apple.

APPLE ORCHARD SPARKLE

SERVES 1

6 ounces apple juice
1 teaspoon simple syrup
½ teaspoon lemon juice
sparkling wine, to top
1 teaspoon granulated sugar, to garnish
1 lemon wedge, to garnish
dried apple slice, to garnish

1. Place the sugar on a small plate or saucer. Rub the rim of a cocktail glass with a lemon wedge, then dip into the sugar and rotate to coat.
2. In a cocktail shaker filled with ice, combine the apple juice, simple syrup, and lemon juice, then shake until the outside of the shaker becomes frosty.
3. Strain into a chilled tumbler and top with sparkling wine. Garnish with a slice of apple.

FRESHLY PICKED

SERVES 1

1 crisp apple
juice of ½ lemon
juice of 1 orange
½ ounce grenadine
1 ounce bourbon

1. Scoop out the center of the apple to form a cup, leaving the base intact. Rub the inside with lemon juice.
2. Discard the core and place the flesh in a blender with the juices, grenadine, bourbon, and ice. Blend until smooth, then pour the mixture into the hollowed apple.

APPLE CINNAMON OLD FASHIONED

SERVES 1

1 tablespoon apple butter
2 ounces bourbon
6 dashes bitters
club soda
cinnamon stick, to garnish
apple slice, to garnish

1. Combine apple butter, bourbon, and bitters in a cocktail shaker and shake well.
2. Pour into a rocks glass and top with club soda. Garnish with a cinnamon stick and an apple slice.

BITE OF THE APPLE

SERVES 2

7½ ounces apple juice
1½ ounces lime juice
1 ounce bourbon
½ teaspoon orgeat syrup
1 tablespoon applesauce or apple puree
ground cinnamon, to garnish

1. Blend together the apple juice, lime juice, bourbon, orgeat syrup, and applesauce with ice until smooth.
2. Pour into a chilled lowball glass and sprinkle with cinnamon.

APPLE BLOSSOM

SERVES 1

2 ounces brandy
1½ ounces apple juice
½ teaspoon lemon juice
lemon slice, to garnish

1. Pour the brandy, apple juice, and lemon juice over ice in a cocktail shaker and shake well.
2. Strain into a chilled cocktail glass and garnish with a slice of lemon.

BLACKBERRY AND APPLE TIPPLE

SERVES 1

1 teaspoon blackberry puree, syrup (page 131), or liqueur
1 ounce apple juice
hard cider, to taste
blackberries, to garnish

1. Place 1 ice cube in the bottom of a champagne flute and add the blackberry puree, syrup, or liqueur.
2. Pour in the apple juice and top with the hard cider to taste. Garnish with a few blackberries.

ARNOLD'S APPLE PALMER

SERVES 1

2 ounces vodka
few dashes Pimm's No. 1
2 ounces apple-infused tea
2 ounces lemonade
apple slices, to garnish

1. In a cocktail shaker filled with ice, combine the first four ingredients, and shake well.
2. Strain into a chilled tall glass. Garnish with apple slices.

THE SAUCY APPLE

SERVES 1

1¾ ounces apple brandy
¾ ounce amaretto
1 teaspoon applesauce
ground cinnamon, to garnish

1. Combine the apple brandy, amaretto, and applesauce in a blender filled with ice.
2. Blend until smooth, then pour the mixture into a chilled cocktail glass. Garnish with a sprinkle of ground cinnamon.

CHAPTER TWO

Pumpkin Spice and Everything Nice

Few things say fall better than pumpkin spice! In this chapter you'll see pumpkin twists on classic cocktails and festive drinks, like a Boozy Pumpkin Spice Latte and a Pumpkin Spice Old Fashioned.

PUMPKIN PIE SPICE

MAKES ABOUT 5½ TABLESPOONS

3 tablespoons ground cinnamon
2 teaspoons ground ginger
2 teaspoons ground nutmeg
1½ teaspoons ground allspice
1½ teaspoons ground cloves

1. In a small bowl, whisk together all spices until well combined.
2. Store in an airtight container. This mixture will stay fresh for at least 6 months.

PUMPKIN SPICE SYRUP

SERVES 16

1½ cups water
½ cup brown sugar
½ cup pumpkin puree
4 teaspoons pumpkin pie spice (page 38)
2 cinnamon sticks, optional

1. Whisk together all ingredients in a pot over low heat until all the sugar has dissolved. Do not let the mixture come to a boil. Let the mixture heat for another 5–6 minutes.
2. Pour the syrup through a mesh strainer, then store in an airtight container. It will keep in the refrigerator for up to 2 weeks. Shake the syrup each time before use.

BOOZY PUMPKIN SPICE LATTE

SERVES 2

12 ounces hot coffee or espresso
¼ cup milk of choice
6 tablespoons pumpkin spice syrup (page 39)
2 ounces bourbon
whipped cream, optional
cinnamon sticks, to garnish
ground cinnamon, to garnish

1. Combine 1 ounce of bourbon with 3 tablespoons of pumpkin spice syrup in each coffee mug. Stir (or use an electric frother) until combined.
2. Heat milk over medium-low heat until it's just beginning to simmer, then remove from heat. Divide milk between both coffee mugs.
3. Add hot coffee or espresso to each mug and stir to combine.
4. Garnish with whipped cream, cinnamon sticks, and ground cinnamon, if desired.

PUMPKIN SPICE MOSCOW MULE

SERVES 1

2 ounces vanilla vodka (or regular vodka)
2 tablespoons pumpkin spice syrup (page 39)
splash of lime juice
ginger beer, for topping
pumpkin pie spice (page 38), to garnish

1. In a cocktail shaker filled with crushed ice, combine vodka, pumpkin spice syrup, and lime juice.
2. Pour into a cocktail glass filled with ice, then top with a few ounces of ginger beer. Garnish with ground pumpkin pie spice.

DRUNKEN PUMPKIN EGGNOG

SERVES 2

2 eggs
½ cup sugar
½ teaspoon pumpkin pie spice (page 38)
3 tablespoons pumpkin puree
¾ cup milk of choice
¾ cup heavy cream
4 ounces brandy or dark rum
nutmeg, to garnish

1. In a blender, blend the eggs on medium speed for 1 minute. Add the sugar and blend for another minute.
2. Add the brandy or rum, pumpkin pie spice, pumpkin puree, milk, and cream, and blend until combined.
3. Place in the refrigerator to chill. When ready to serve, give the mixture a stir, then pour into 2 glasses. Garnish with ground nutmeg.

PUMPKIN SPICE MARTINI

SERVES 1

1½ ounces vanilla vodka
1½ ounces Irish cream liqueur
1 ounce pumpkin spice syrup (page 39)
cinnamon stick, to garnish

1. In a cocktail shaker filled with ice, shake together the vanilla vodka, Irish cream liqueur, and pumpkin spice syrup.
2. Strain into a martini glass. Garnish with a cinnamon stick.

PUMPKIN SPICE OLD FASHIONED

SERVES 1

2 ounces bourbon
1 tablespoon pumpkin puree
1 tablespoon maple syrup
¼ teaspoon pumpkin pie spice (page 38)
¼ teaspoon vanilla
1 dash Angostura bitters
cinnamon stick, to garnish

1. In a cocktail shaker filled with ice, shake together all ingredients until cold.
2. Strain into a lowball glass filled with a few ice cubes, and garnish with a cinnamon stick.

SPICED PUMPKIN SMASH

SERVES 1

2–4 tablespoons pumpkin spice syrup (page 39)
2 ounces whiskey
½ ounce orange juice
1–2 dashes orange bitters
ginger beer, for topping
cinnamon stick, to garnish
orange peel, to garnish

1. In a cocktail shaker filled with ice, shake together the first four ingredients until cold.
2. Strain into a lowball glass and top with ginger beer. Garnish with a cinnamon stick and an orange peel.

WHITE PUMPKIN ESPRESSO MARTINI

SERVES 1

2 ounces vodka
½ ounce coffee liqueur
1 ounce brewed espresso, cooled
2 tablespoons pumpkin spice syrup (page 39)
frothed heavy cream, for topping
coffee beans, to garnish

1. In a cocktail shaker, combine vodka, coffee liqueur, espresso, and pumpkin spice syrup, and shake until frothy.
2. Pour into a chilled cocktail glass, top with frothed heavy cream, and garnish with a few coffee beans.

THE RUSSIAN PUMPKIN

SERVES 1

1 ounce vodka
1 ounce coffee liqueur
2 ounces heavy cream
½ teaspoon pumpkin pie spice (page 38), plus extra to garnish
cinnamon stick, to garnish

1. In a cocktail shaker filled with ice, combine vodka, coffee liqueur, heavy cream, and pumpkin pie spice. Shake until well mixed.
2. Pour into a lowball cocktail glass. Garnish with a sprinkle of pumpkin pie spice and a cinnamon stick.

CHAPTER THREE

October is BOO-zy season! This chapter provides a truly fun collection of spooky-inspired cocktails, perfect for your next Halloween party or when a witch simply needs a drink after a long day.

WITCH-TINI

SERVES 1

¾ ounce vodka
¾ ounce sour apple schnapps
¾ ounce apple juice
apple wedge, to garnish

1. In a cocktail shaker filled with ice, combine the vodka, apple schnapps, and apple juice. Shake until well frosted.
2. Strain into a chilled martini glass and garnish the glass with an apple wedge.

CORPSE REVIVER

SERVES 1

2 ounces brandy
1 ounce apple brandy
1 ounce sweet vermouth

1. In a mixing glass, pour the brandy, apple brandy, and vermouth over ice. Stir gently to mix.
2. Strain into a chilled cocktail glass.

THE POISONED APPLE

SERVES 1

2 ounces apple brandy
1 ounce apple juice or apple cider

1. In a cocktail shaker filled with ice, combine the apple brandy and apple juice or cider. Shake until well frosted.
2. Strain into a chilled cocktail glass.

CRIMSON CAULDRON

SERVES 1

2 ounces rye whiskey
1 ounce grapefruit juice
1 teaspoon grenadine

1. In a cocktail shaker filled with ice, combine all ingredients and shake until well frosted.
2. Strain into a chilled cocktail glass.

PHANTOM PUNCH

SERVES 8

5 ounces bourbon, chilled
5 ounces limoncello, chilled
5 ounces amaretto, chilled
1¾ ounces grenadine
2 cups apple cider, chilled
2 cups orange juice, chilled
2 oranges, sliced
2 apples, sliced
3½ ounces dry ice pellets

WARNING

Dry ice is a hazardous substance and can cause severe burns if it comes into contact with skin and eyes. Ensure protective gloves, such as oven mitts, are always worn when handling the ice, as well as any tools or containers in contact with it. Do not leave dry ice unattended around children. Do not store dry ice in an airtight container and always use in a well-ventilated area. Always read the instructions supplied with dry ice. Dry ice has a short shelf life, so make sure it's readily available for day-of use.

1. Mix the bourbon, limoncello, amaretto, grenadine, apple cider, and orange juice in a large punch bowl. Add the orange and apple slices.

2. Place the punch bowl in a large, deep tray filled with water.

3. When using dry ice, use oven mitts and a scoop when transferring the pellets evenly into the water. Serve the punch immediately. The foggy effect will last for only about 5 minutes. Once it has cleared, simply add some more dry ice to the water in the tray.

WITCH'S BREW

SERVES 2

2 ounces brewed black tea
2 ounces dark rum
1 cup orange juice
½ cup fresh lemon juice
sugar, to taste
orange slices, to garnish

1. Combine the tea, rum, orange juice, and lemon juice in a saucepan over medium-low heat.
2. Once the mixture is warm, pour into heatproof mugs and sweeten to taste. Garnish with orange slices.

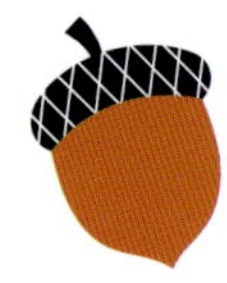

MIDNIGHT ELIXIR

SERVES 1

2½ ounces gin
¾ ounce blue curaçao

1. In a cocktail shaker filled with ice, combine the gin and curaçao and shake until well frosted. Strain into a chilled cocktail glass.

SPOOKY SOUR

SERVES 1

1¾ ounces light rum
½ ounce guava juice
½ ounce lemon juice
½ ounce orange juice

1. Blend the light rum, guava juice, lemon juice, and orange juice with ice until it's a slushy consistency.
2. Pour the mixture into a chilled martini glass.

DARK SIDE OF THE MOON

SERVES 1

2 ounces black sambuca, chilled
2 ounces dry vermouth, chilled
club soda, to taste

1. In a cocktail shaker filled with ice, combine the black sambuca and dry vermouth. Shake well.
2. Strain into a rocks glass and top with club soda to taste.

THE GREEN MONSTER

SERVES 1

¾ ounce light rum
½ ounce blue curaçao
¾ ounce orange juice
lime wedge, to garnish
confectioners' sugar, to garnish
lime slice, to garnish

1. Place the confectioners' sugar on a small plate or saucer. Rub the rim of a cocktail glass with a lime wedge, then dip in the sugar and rotate to coat.
2. In a cocktail shaker filled with ice, combine the light rum, blue curaçao, and orange juice, and shake until well frosted.
3. Pour into a chilled cocktail glass and garnish with a slice of lime.

CHAPTER FOUR

Whether you've been playing in a pile of leaves or picking out a perfect pumpkin, these heated drinks offer a hint of brandy or rum to help you warm up after being outside on a brisk autumn day.

BOURBON APPLE CIDER

SERVES 10

½ gallon apple cider
2–3 cups bourbon
1 apple, sliced, reserve some to garnish
1 pear, sliced, reserve some to garnish
16 cinnamon sticks
10 fresh rosemary sprigs, to garnish

1. In a large pot, combine apple cider, bourbon, apple and pear slices, and 6 cinnamon sticks, and heat on medium-low for 10 minutes.
2. Reduce to low heat to keep warm. Garnish with reserved apple and pear slices, cinnamon sticks, and a sprig of fresh rosemary, and serve warm.

APPLE TODDY

SERVES 2

2 ounces whiskey, rum, or brandy
6 ounces hard apple cider
lemon slices, to garnish

1. Warm the spirit and cider together in a saucepan over medium heat.
2. After a few minutes, pour the warm mixture into 2 heatproof glasses. Garnish each with a slice of lemon.

HARVEST MOON

SERVES 1

4 ounces apple cider
1 tablespoon brown sugar
pinch of ground cinnamon
pinch of freshly grated nutmeg
2 ounces apple brandy
whipped cream, for topping

1. Combine the apple cider, brown sugar, cinnamon, and nutmeg in a saucepan over medium-low heat. Heat gently, stirring until the sugar has dissolved.
2. Pour into a heatproof glass and stir in the apple brandy. Top with whipped cream.

HOT PUMPKIN PIE

SERVES 2

8 ounces milk of choice
4 ounces Irish cream liqueur
1 ounce vanilla or pumpkin spice vodka
½ cup pumpkin puree
¼ tablespoon pumpkin pie spice (page 38)
whipped cream, for topping
cinnamon, to garnish

1. In a large pot over medium-high heat, combine the milk, Irish cream liqueur, and vodka.
2. Once mixture is just starting to simmer, turn the heat to low. Whisk in pumpkin puree and pumpkin pie spice until combined.
3. Pour warm mixture into heatproof glasses, top with whipped cream, and garnish with a sprinkle of cinnamon.

HOT CARAMEL LATTE

SERVES 2

¼ cup granulated sugar
⅓ cup water
1¼ cups milk
½ cup hot espresso
1¾ ounces alcohol of choice (bourbon, rum, Irish cream liqueur, coffee liqueur, etc.)

1. To make the caramel, put the sugar and 2 tablespoons of the water into a small, heavy saucepan. Heat gently until the sugar dissolves, then boil rapidly for 4–5 minutes, without stirring, until the mixture turns to a golden caramel.
2. Remove from the heat and carefully pour in the remaining water. Stir until the caramel dissolves, then return the pan to the heat and simmer for an additional 3–4 minutes, until syrupy.
3. Put the milk into a separate saucepan and heat over medium heat until almost boiling. Remove from the heat, pour in the espresso, alcohol, and almost all the caramel sauce, and whisk until frothy. Divide between 2 tall latte glasses.
4. Drizzle the remaining caramel sauce over the top.

SPIKED ORANGE HOT CHOCOLATE

SERVES 4-6

3 cups milk
1 cup heavy cream
½ cup sugar
¼ cup unsweetened cocoa powder
kosher salt
6 ounces orange-flavored milk chocolate, chopped
1 teaspoon pure vanilla extract
4 ounces alcohol of choice (bourbon, rum, Irish cream liqueur, coffee liqueur, etc.)

1. Combine the milk, heavy cream, sugar, cocoa powder, and a pinch of salt in a saucepan. Cook over medium heat, stirring occasionally, until the sugar and cocoa powder dissolve and the milk is steaming. Be careful not to bring to a boil.

2. Whisk in half of the chopped chocolate until melted, then whisk in the remaining chocolate until combined.

3. Remove from the heat, whisk in the vanilla and your alcohol of choice, and pour into mugs.

SALTED CARAMEL RUM HOT COCOA

SERVES 4

2 tablespoons granulated sugar
1 tablespoon water
salt flakes
7 ounces milk
1½ ounces semisweet chocolate, broken into pieces
1 teaspoon unsweetened cocoa powder
pinch ground cinnamon
¾ ounce dark rum
shaved or grated semisweet chocolate, to garnish
mini marshmallows, to serve

1. Add the sugar and water to a small heavy saucepan and heat gently, without stirring, until the sugar has completely dissolved.
2. Bring to a boil and boil rapidly, without stirring, until the simple syrup begins to turn golden around the edges. Keep a very close eye on it at this stage and continue to heat until the syrup has turned to caramel.
3. Remove the pan from the heat, add the salt, swirl to mix, then gradually pour in the milk. Put the pan back over low heat and stir to mix the caramel and milk together. Add the chocolate. Stir the cocoa powder with a little water to make a paste and add it with the cinnamon. Keep stirring until smooth.
4. When the chocolate mix is hot but not boiling, stir in the rum, warm together, then pour into 4 heatproof glass mugs. Sprinkle with shaved or grated chocolate. Add mini marshmallows, if desired.

MULLED MARSALA

SERVES 8

1 bottle marsala wine
16 ounces water
6 cloves
4 ounces amaretto
¼ cup granulated sugar
orange slices, to garnish
star anise, to garnish

1. In a pot over medium-high heat, combine the marsala, water, and cloves. Heat until the mixture is almost boiling.
2. Remove from the heat, add the sugar, and stir to dissolve. Serve in heatproof glasses, and garnish with an orange slice and star anise.

SPIKED CINNAMON TEA

SERVES 2

12 ounces water
4 cloves
1 small cinnamon stick
2 bags black tea
3½ ounces spiced rum
lemon juice, to taste
brown sugar, to taste
lemon slices, to garnish

1. Bring the water, cloves, and cinnamon stick to a boil.
2. Remove from the heat and add the tea bags. Steep for 5 minutes, then remove the tea bags.
3. Stir in the spiced rum, then add the lemon juice and brown sugar to taste.
4. Strain into heatproof glasses. Garnish with a lemon slice.

RUM ESPRESSO WITH WHIPPED CREAM

SERVES 4

⅔ cup heavy cream
1¼ cups hot espresso
1 tablespoon rum
2 teaspoons raw sugar, plus extra for sprinkling

1. Pour the heavy cream into a bowl and whip until it holds soft peaks.
2. Mix the espresso, rum, and sugar in a liquid measuring cup and pour into 4 small heatproof glasses or coffee cups.
3. Gently drop spoonfuls of the cream into the espresso. Sprinkle with a little extra sugar and serve.

CHAPTER FIVE

Here you'll find cocktails full of spice, perfect for sipping on while carving pumpkins, watching favorite fall films, or baking festive desserts. These recipes feature warm and nutty notes that infuse each cocktail with autumnal flavors.

RUM NOGGIN

SERVES 8

6 eggs
4–5 teaspoons confectioners' sugar
freshly grated nutmeg, plus extra for sprinkling
16 ounces (2 cups) dark rum
5 cups milk, warmed

1. Whisk the eggs in a punch bowl with the sugar and a little nutmeg.
2. Whisk in the rum and gradually stir in the milk.
3. Warm through gently, if desired, and serve in heatproof glasses or mugs, and sprinkle with nutmeg.

SPICED AUTUMN SOUR

SERVES 1

¾ ounce gin
¾ ounce sherry
¾ ounce bourbon
¾ ounce lemon juice
¾ ounce spiced syrup
1 egg white

SPICED SYRUP
½ cinnamon stick
2 star anise
6 black peppercorns
1⅔ cups granulated sugar
5 ounces water

1. To make the spiced syrup, gently heat all the ingredients in a saucepan over low heat until all sugar has dissolved.

2. Remove from the heat and let cool, then strain and pour into a bottle. The syrup will keep in the refrigerator for up to 1 month.

3. To make the cocktail, put the gin, sherry, bourbon, lemon juice, spiced syrup, and egg white into a cocktail shaker. Dry shake all the ingredients. Add a handful of ice cubes and shake vigorously for 30 seconds to create a foam.

4. Double strain into a lowball cocktail glass.

PEARTINI

SERVES 1

¾ ounce vodka
1 ounce pear brandy
1 teaspoon granulated sugar, to garnish
pinch ground cinnamon, to garnish
1 lemon wedge, to garnish

1. Mix the sugar and cinnamon in a saucer. Rub the rim of a cocktail glass with the lemon wedge, then dip in the cinnamon sugar mixture and rotate to coat.
2. In a cocktail shaker filled with ice, combine the vodka and pear brandy. Shake well and strain into a martini glass.

CINNAMON SPICE CREAM

SERVES 1

1¾ ounces golden rum
1¼ ounces brandy
1 teaspoon simple syrup
4 ounces milk
ground cinnamon, to garnish
cinnamon stick, to garnish

1. Put the rum, brandy, simple syrup, and milk into a blender with crushed ice and blend until well combined.
2. Pour into a chilled cocktail glass. Sprinkle with ground cinnamon and garnish with a cinnamon stick.

PLUM & GINGER WHISKEY FIZZ

SERVES 1

1¾ ounces plum & ginger whiskey
¾ ounce lemon juice
club soda, for topping
lemon slice, to garnish

PLUM & GINGER WHISKEY
6 ripe plums, coarsely chopped
large piece fresh ginger, peeled and sliced
2 tablespoons granulated sugar
3 whole cloves
1½ cups whiskey

1. This cocktail takes 1 week to infuse. Put the plums, ginger, sugar, and cloves into a saucepan. Place over low heat and cook for 5 minutes. Let cool.

2. Pour the mixture into a sealable jar, then add the the whiskey. Stir the mixture, seal the jar, and store in a cool place. Let flavors infuse and develop for 1 week. Once infused, the whiskey can be stored and used for up to 2 months. After 1 week, pour the whiskey through a fine strainer.

3. To make the cocktail, combine the whiskey and lemon juice into a cocktail shaker filled with ice. Shake until well frosted.

4. Pour into a highball glass filled with ice. Top with club soda and garnish with a lemon slice.

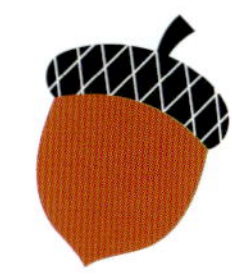

SWEET AND SPICED

SERVES 1

1 egg
2 teaspoons confectioners' sugar
½ teaspoon grated nutmeg, plus extra to garnish
2 ounces rum, port, brandy, or whiskey

1. Whisk the egg, sugar, and nutmeg together.
2. Warm the rum in a saucepan over a low heat, then whisk in the egg mixture.
3. Serve in a heatproof glass when mixture has warmed. Do not warm for too long or the egg can curdle. Add nutmeg to garnish.

MATCHA VODKA REFRESHER

SERVES 1

1¾ ounces matcha vodka
1 teaspoon honey
1 teaspoon lemon juice
¾ ounce apple cider
1 small cinnamon stick, to garnish

MATCHA VODKA
1½ cups vodka
1 teaspoon matcha green tea powder
2 small cinnamon sticks

1. To make the matcha vodka, pour vodka into a sterilized, sealable jar, then add the matcha green tea powder and cinnamon sticks. Stir the mixture, seal the jar, and let stand in a cool place for 24 hours.
2. After 24 hours, remove the cinnamon sticks and strain through a fine strainer. Pour the infused vodka into an airtight container. This vodka can be stored for up to 2 months.
3. Put 1¾ ounces of the infused vodka into a cocktail shaker filled with ice. Add the honey, lemon juice, and apple cider.
4. Shake until well frosted, then strain the cocktail into the glass. Garnish with a cinnamon stick.

CHAPTER SIX

Inspired by the German celebration that runs from the end of September to the beginning of October, this section is filled with traditional Oktoberfest flavors and drinks like Glühwein, Alsterwasser, and, of course, lots of beer.

ALSTERWASSER

SERVES 1

8 ounces sparkling lemonade, chilled
8 ounces pale lager, chilled
slice of lemon, to garnish

1. Fill a pint glass halfway with sparkling lemonade, then fill the rest of the glass with your lager of choice.
2. Garnish with a thin slice of lemon.

GLÜHWEIN

SERVES 12

3 bottles red wine
grated peel of 1 lemon
grated peel of 1 orange
pinch of ground ginger, cinnamon, and cloves
½ cup granulated sugar
cinnamon sticks, to garnish
orange peel curls, to garnish

1. Heat the wine in a saucepan over medium-low heat along with the lemon and orange peels, spices, and sugar.
2. When the sugar has completely dissolved and the wine is hot, remove from the heat and let sit for 5–10 minutes.
3. Dilute with water to taste. Serve in heatproof glasses with a cinnamon stick and an orange peel curl.

GINGER BEER

SERVES 1

1 cup beer
2 ounces ginger brandy

1. Pour the beer into a chilled beer glass or tankard, then add the ginger brandy.

GERMAN MULE

SERVES 1

2 ounces herbal liqueur, like Jägermeister
1 ounce lime juice
4 ounces ginger beer
mint leaves, to garnish
orange slice, to garnish
cinnamon stick, to garnish

1. Fill a copper mug with ice and pour in the herbal liqueur and lime juice.
2. Top with ginger beer and gently stir.
3. Garnish with fresh mint leaves, an orange slice, and a cinnamon stick.

BOILERMAKER

SERVES 1

1 cup pale ale, chilled
1½ ounces bourbon or rye whiskey

1. Pour the ale into a chilled beer glass or tankard.
2. Pour the bourbon or rye into a shot glass. Then gently submerge the shot glass of bourbon or whiskey into the beer.

HUNDENASE

SERVES 1

1 cup pale ale
1 ounce gin

1. Pour the ale into a chilled beer glass, then pour in the gin.

BLACKBERRY RADLER

SERVES 2

16 ounces sparkling lemonade, chilled
2 tablespoons blackberry syrup
16 ounces German lager, chilled
lemon slice, to garnish
blackberries, to garnish

BLACKBERRY SYRUP
3 cups blackberries
1 cup granulated sugar
1 tablespoon lemon juice
1 cup water

1. To make the blackberry syrup, add all ingredients to a pan over medium heat and bring to a boil, stirring occasionally, for 2 minutes. Remove from heat and cool. Smash the blackberries with the back of a spoon, then strain before storing. Store in an airtight container in the refrigerator for up to 2 weeks.
2. Fill 2 pint glasses halfway with sparkling lemonade and 2 tablespoons of blackberry syrup, and gently stir to combine.
3. Fill the rest of the glasses with your lager of choice.
4. Garnish with a slice of lemon and a few blackberries.

THE BOOZY BAVARIAN

Serves 1

4 ounces freshly brewed coffee
½ ounce peppermint schnapps
½ ounce coffee liqueur
1 ounce half-and-half
1 teaspoon granulated sugar
whipped cream, for topping

1. Combine the first five ingredients in a coffee mug and stir until mixed well.
2. Top with whipped cream.

APPLE BEER PUNCH

SERVES 6–8

4 large apples, cored and thinly sliced
2 cups granulated sugar
juice of 1 lemon
6 cinnamon sticks
6 whole cloves
6 (12-ounce) bottles of German lager
3 lemons, sliced

1. In a large pot over medium-high heat, combine the apple slices, sugar, lemon juice, cinnamon sticks, and cloves, and bring to a boil.
2. Lower the heat and simmer, stirring occasionally, until all the sugar has dissolved. Remove from heat and let cool.
3. Pour cooled mixture into a large punch bowl, then add the lager and lemon slices. Stir to combine.
4. Keep the punch refrigerated until ready to serve.

BAVARIAN ORANGE FIZZ

SERVES 1

2–3 tablespoons orange juice
lager, chilled
champagne, chilled
orange slice, to garnish

1. Pour the orange juice into the bottom of a cocktail glass.
2. Slowly add equal quantities of lager and champagne, and garnish with an orange slice.

CHAPTER SEVEN

The sun is setting and everyone is wearing their coziest sweaters, ready to hang around the bonfire with a drink. The cocktails in this chapter feature smoky flavors, with some drinks inspired by the best bonfire snack—s'mores!

S'MORES COFFEE

SERVES 4

¾ cup heavy cream
3 cups black coffee
6 ounces milk chocolate or semisweet chocolate, chopped
4 ounces alcohol of choice (bourbon, rum, Irish cream liqueur, coffee liqueur, etc.)
marshmallows, to garnish
warm chocolate sauce, to garnish
chocolate shavings, to garnish

1. Heat the heavy cream and coffee in a saucepan until almost boiling. Turn the heat to low and stir in the chopped chocolate. Whisk until the chocolate has completely melted.

2. Remove from the heat and stir in the alcohol. Pour into 4 heatproof glasses on a baking tray.

3. Preheat the broiler. Add marshmallows to each glass and place the tray under the preheated broiler for about 1 minute, until the marshmallows begin to brown and melt. Let each mug cool until it reaches a temperature that's still warm but safe to drink.

4. Drizzle the chocolate sauce over the marshmallows and sprinkle with the chocolate shavings.

SMOKED GIN SWIZZLE

SERVES 1

1 ounce smoked gin
¾ ounce lime juice
2 teaspoons granulated sugar
1 teaspoon Angostura bitters
6 ounces club soda
lime slice, to garnish

SMOKED GIN
3½ ounces whiskey barrel wood chips
1½ cups gin

1. This cocktail takes 2 weeks to infuse. To make the smoked gin, lay the wood chips on a metal tray, then place the tray on a heatproof surface. Scorch the wood chips with a chef's blowtorch until about half are blackened. Put the wood chips into a sealable jar, then pour in the gin. Stir the mixture, seal the jar, and store in a cool place.

3. After 2 weeks, pour the gin through a fine strainer. Combine the smoked gin, lime juice, sugar, and bitters into a highball glass filled with crushed ice.

4. Top with the club soda and serve with a lime slice.

BONFIRE PUNCH

SERVES 15

32 ounces bourbon
1 bottle red wine
4½ cups brewed black tea
2 cups dark rum
1 cup gin
1 cup apricot brandy
3½ ounces lemon juice
3½ ounces lime juice
4 tablespoons simple syrup
orange slices, to garnish

1. Pour the first nine ingredients into a large bowl and mix. Refrigerate for 2 hours.
2. When ready to serve, pour the punch into a large punch bowl filled with ice and garnish with orange slices.

SMOKED LAST WORD

SERVES 1

1 ounce smoked gin
¾ ounce lime juice
¾ ounce maraschino liqueur
¾ ounce green Chartreuse
lime slice, to garnish

SMOKED GIN
3½ ounces whiskey barrel wood chips
1½ cups gin

1. This cocktail takes 2 weeks to infuse. To make the smoked gin, lay the wood chips on a metal tray, then place the tray on a heatproof surface. Scorch the wood chips with a chef's blowtorch until about half are blackened. Put the wood chips into a sealable jar, then pour in the gin. Stir the mixture, seal the jar, and store in a cool place. After 2 weeks, pour the gin through a strainer.
2. To make the cocktail, combine the smoked gin, lime juice, maraschino liqueur, green Chartreuse in a cocktail shaker filled with ice.
3. Shake well and double strain into a coupe glass. Garnish with the lime slice.

THE BOOZY S'MORE

SERVES 1

1 ounce chocolate liqueur
1 ounce vanilla vodka (or regular vodka)
½ ounce heavy cream
2 tablespoons marshmallow creme
chocolate syrup, to garnish
graham crackers, crushed, to garnish
toasted marshmallow, to garnish

1. Place crushed graham crackers on a small plate or saucer, then pour chocolate syrup on another plate or saucer. Dip the rim in the chocolate syrup, then dip in the graham crackers and rotate to coat.

2. Pour the chocolate liqueur into the glass.

3. In a small bowl, whisk together the vodka, heavy cream, and marshmallow creme.

4. Slowly pour the vodka mixture over the back of a spoon and into the glass. This should create a layered effect.

5. Garnish with a toasted marshmallow on a cocktail skewer.

BONFIRE OLD FASHIONED

SERVES 1

1½ ounces whiskey
1 tablespoon maple syrup
3 dashes chocolate bitters
toasted marshmallows, to garnish

1. Pour whiskey, maple syrup, and bitters into a rocks glass filled with ice.
2. Stir until well combined, then garnish with toasted marshmallows on a cocktail skewer.

RUM COBBLER

SERVES 1

1 ounce smoked rum
splash grenadine
½ ounce maraschino liqueur
cocktail cherry, to garnish
orange slices, to garnish
lime slices, to garnish

SMOKED RUM
3½ ounces whiskey barrel wood chips
1½ cups rum

1. This cocktail takes 2 weeks to infuse. To make the smoked rum, lay the wood chips on a metal tray, then place the tray on a heatproof surface. Scorch the wood chips with a chef's blowtorch until about half are blackened. Put the wood chips into a sealable jar, then pour in the rum. Stir the mixture, seal the jar, and store in a cool place. After 2 weeks, pour the rum through a strainer.
2. To make the cocktail, pour the rum into an old-fashioned glass filled with ice.
3. Add the grenadine and maraschino liqueur and stir. Garnish with the cherry, orange, and lime.

BONFIRE CIDER SMASH

Serves 1

¾ ounce whiskey
hard cider, for topping
few dashes Angostura bitters

1. Stir the whiskey with ice in a tall glass.
2. Top off with cider to taste and finish with a few dashes of Angostura bitters.

HAZELNUT VODKA ESPRESSO

Serves 1

¾ ounce brewed espresso
1¾ ounces Frangelico or hazelnut liqueur
½ ounce vodka
½ teaspoon granulated sugar
1 marshmallow
½ ounce rum

1. Pour the espresso, Frangelico, vodka, and sugar into a cocktail shaker filled with ice. Shake until well frosted. Strain into a heatproof glass.
2. Float the marshmallow on top of the cocktail, then gently pour the rum over the marshmallow.
3. Ignite the marshmallow using a long match or lighter. Let the flames die down completely and check that the marshmallow and glass have cooled before drinking.

THE TOASTED MARSHMALLOW

SERVES 1

1½ ounces Irish cream liqueur
½ ounce marshmallow vodka
½ ounce brewed espresso, cooled
1 tablespoon brown sugar, to garnish
toasted marshmallow, to garnish

1. Place brown sugar on a small plate or saucer. Wet the outside rim of a martini glass with water, then dip in the brown sugar and rotate to coat.

2. In a cocktail shaker filled with ice, add Irish cream liqueur, marshmallow vodka, and espresso. Shake well to combine.

3. Strain the drink into the martini glass and garnish with a toasted marshmallow on a cocktail skewer.

CHAPTER EIGHT

There's nothing like the smell of an apple or pumpkin pie baking in the oven on a cool fall day. Inspired by favorite fall desserts, these sweet cocktails pack a little extra boozy kick.

APPLE PIE CREAM

SERVES 1

3½ ounces hard apple cider
1 small scoop vanilla ice cream
club soda
cinnamon sugar, to garnish
apple, to garnish

1. Add the apple cider and ice cream to a blender filled with a handful of ice.
2. Blend for 10–15 seconds, until frothy and frosted. Pour into a glass and top with club soda.
3. Garnish with a sprinkle of cinnamon sugar and an apple slice.

PUMPKIN PIE ON THE ROCKS

SERVES 2

4 ounces pumpkin sauce
4 ounces milk of choice
2 ounces dark rum
2 ounces vanilla vodka
1 tablespoon simple syrup, to garnish
2 tablespoons graham crackers, crushed, to garnish

PUMPKIN SAUCE
½ cup pumpkin puree
½ cup water
¼ cup brown sugar, lightly packed
1 teaspoon pumpkin pie spice (page 38)
1 teaspoon vanilla extract
¼ teaspoon salt

1. To make the pumpkin sauce, combine all ingredients in a saucepan over medium heat and bring to a simmer, stirring occasionally. Heat for 5–7 minutes until mixture has reduced to about ½ cup and sugar has dissolved. Remove from heat and transfer to a bowl to cool completely before using.
2. Place crushed graham crackers on a small plate or saucer, then pour the simple syrup on another plate or saucer. Dip the rim of each glass in the simple syrup, then dip in the graham crackers and rotate to coat.
3. In a cocktail shaker filled with ice, add the cooled pumpkin sauce, milk, rum, and vodka. Shake until well combined.
4. Strain the mixture equally into each glass filled with ice.

DRUNKEN CUSTARD DELIGHT

SERVES 4

12 ounces condensed milk
10 ounces milk
4 egg yolks
¼ teaspoon vanilla extract
2½ ounces vodka
sprinkle of cinnamon, to garnish
1 cinnamon stick, to garnish

1. Mix the milks, egg yolks, vanilla extract, and vodka in a blender on high speed for 45 seconds.
2. Strain and leave in the refrigerator until cooled.
3. Pour the cocktail into glasses, and garnish with a sprinkle of cinnamon and a cinnamon stick.

TIPSY CARAMEL APPLE

SERVES 1

2 ounces bourbon
1 tablespoon caramel sauce
juice of ½ lemon
few dashes Angostura bitters
2 ounces hard apple cider or non-alcoholic apple cider
apple slices, to garnish

1. In a cocktail shaker filled with ice, combine bourbon, caramel sauce, and lemon juice. Shake until well combined.

2. Pour the mixture into a cocktail glass filled with ice. Add a few dashes of Angostura bitters, then top with the apple cider. Garnish with apple slices.

PUMPKIN CHEESECAKE-TINI

SERVES 1

3 tablespoons pumpkin puree
2 tablespoons brown sugar cinnamon syrup
2 ounces vanilla vodka
1 ounce half-and-half
½ ounce amaro liqueur
½ ounce spiced rum
¼ teaspoon pumpkin pie spice (page 38), reserve a pinch to garnish
whipped cream, to garnish

1. In a cocktail shaker filled with ice, combine the pumpkin puree, brown sugar cinnamon syrup, vodka, half-and-half, amaro, rum, and pumpkin pie spice, reserving a pinch for the garnish. Shake until well frosted.
2. Strain into a martini glass. Garnish with whipped cream and a pinch of pumpkin pie spice.

PLASTERED PECAN PIE

SERVES 2

2 tablespoons maple syrup
2 ounces bourbon
2 ounces praline pecan liqueur
1½ ounces heavy cream
whipped cream, for topping
maple syrup, to garnish
2 tablespoons toasted pecan halves, crushed, to garnish, reserve uncrushed halves for additional garnish

1. Place crushed pecans on a small plate or saucer, then spread the maple syrup on another plate or saucer. Dip the rim of each cocktail glass in the maple syrup, then dip in the crushed pecans and rotate to coat.
2. In a cocktail shaker, combine maple syrup, bourbon, praline pecan liqueur, and heavy cream. Shake until well combined.
3. Strain equally into 2 glasses filled with ice. Garnish with whipped cream and pecan halves.

APPLE STRUDEL COCKTAIL

SERVES 1

1 ounce spiced rum
½ ounce cinnamon syrup
½ ounce white rum
½ ounce lemon juice
2 ounces apple cider
apple slice, to garnish
fresh rosemary sprig, to garnish

1. In a cocktail shaker filled with ice, combine all liquid ingredients and shake until well combined.
2. Strain into a cocktail glass filled with ice. Garnish with an apple slice and sprig of rosemary.

CHAPTER NINE

Among this collection of fall flavors, you'll find some festive and delicious recipes that pair well with the cocktails included in this book. From appetizers to seasonal snacks to warm desserts, there's bound to be something for everyone to enjoy with their drink of choice.

CHEESY STUFFED MUSHROOMS

SERVES 4 | PREP: 15 MINS | COOK: 5 MINS

2 pounds portobello mushrooms
⅓ cup olive oil
1 teaspoon salt
1 teaspoon pepper
4 garlic cloves, chopped
small bunch of fresh parsley, chopped
1 pound gorgonzola, cut in thin slices

1. Prep the grill on high heat.
2. Once the stems have been removed, drizzle the inside of the mushrooms with olive oil, then sprinkle salt, pepper, garlic, and parsley on each. Top each mushroom with a few strips of cheese.
3. Place on the grill rack and cook, cheese side up, with the lid on for 5 minutes until the mushrooms are cooked and the cheese has melted. These can be made in advance and kept in the refrigerator for up to a day.

HONEY SPICED NUTS

SERVES 6 | PREP: 5 MINS | BAKE: 10 MINS

A few handfuls of these spiced nuts are sure to pair beautifully with a glass of Spiked Cinnamon Tea (page 97) or a Bourbon Apple Cider (page 81).

½ cup Brazil nuts
½ cup pecans
½ cup cashew nuts
2 tablespoons pumpkin seeds
1 tablespoon sunflower oil
1½ tablespoons honey, divided
½ teaspoon ground cinnamon
½ teaspoon allspice
½ teaspoon black pepper
½ teaspoon sweet paprika
¼ teaspoon salt

1. Line a baking sheet with parchment paper and preheat the oven to 275°F.
2. Reserving half of the honey for later, combine all ingredients in a bowl and mix. Then spread the mixture on the prepared baking sheet.
3. Place on the middle shelf of the oven and cook for 10 minutes. Remove from the oven, then drizzle the remaining honey over the nuts. Let cool before serving. Store in an airtight container for up to a week.

ROASTED FIGS WITH HONEY & THYME

SERVES 4 | PREP: 10 MINS | BAKE: 20 MINS

8 figs
10 sprigs of fresh thyme, broken into pieces
½ cup honey
½ cup plain Greek yogurt, to serve, optional

1. Preheat the oven to 350°F. Cut a deep X shape through each fig, stopping just before it reaches the bottom, and stuff it with 2 pieces of thyme.

2. Line a small roasting pan with parchment paper, letting it come up the sides. Put the figs on the paper, drizzle a tablespoon of honey onto each fig, then sprinkle with the remaining thyme.

3. Roast the figs for 20 minutes. Serve hot with the syrup in the parchment paper and a generous spoonful of yogurt, if using.

AUTUMN TRAIL MIX

SERVES 6 | PREP: 10 MINS, PLUS COOLING | BAKE: 8–10 MINS

2¼ cups almonds
3 tablespoons pine nuts
3 tablespoons pumpkin seeds
3 tablespoons sunflower seeds
⅔ cup dried banana chips
2 dates, pitted and coarsely chopped
2 tablespoons oat bran
½ teaspoon ground allspice
1 medium egg white

1. Preheat the oven to 400°F. Combine all ingredients, except the egg white, in a large bowl and mix well.

2. Lightly beat the egg white with a fork in a small bowl, then add to the nut mixture, stirring to coat all the ingredients evenly.

3. Spread the mixture out in a single layer on a large baking sheet. Bake in the preheated oven for 8–10 minutes until crisp and lightly browned.

4. Let cool completely before serving. The trail mix will keep for up to 5 days stored in an airtight container.

CARAMELIZED APPLE SLICES

SERVES 4 | PREP: 15 MINS | BAKE: 5–6 MINS

4 crisp sweet apples
juice of ½ lemon
3 tablespoons brown sugar
¼ teaspoon ground cinnamon
2 tablespoons butter, melted
vanilla ice cream or whipped cream, optional, to serve

1. Prep the grill on high heat.
2. Remove a thin slice from the top and bottom of the apples. Remove the cores, then slice each apple into 3 thick rings. Put into a bowl and toss with lemon juice to prevent discoloration.
3. Mix the brown sugar and cinnamon in another bowl, then sprinkle the mix over the apples. Drizzle the melted butter over the apples.
4. Place the apples on the grill rack and cook for 5–6 minutes until golden and slightly charred, turning every 2 minutes. Transfer to bowls and serve with ice cream or whipped cream.

BOOZY PEARS

SERVES 8 | PREP: 15 MINS | BAKE: 15-20 MINS

These boozy pears go perfectly with an equally boozy Peartini (page 106) or a Rum Noggin (page 102).

8 pears, halved and seeded
4 tablespoons butter, plus extra for greasing
3 tablespoons brown sugar
few drops amaretto liqueur (can also use cognac or brandy)
vanilla ice cream, to serve

1. Prep the grill to medium-low heat. Brush 8 pieces of aluminum foil with butter.
2. Place 2 pear halves on each piece of foil. Top each pear half with a small pat of butter, a sprinkle of brown sugar, and a few drops of the amaretto liqueur. Wrap the foil into a loose package, sealing well.
3. Place on the grill rack and cook with the lid on for 15–20 minutes until tender. Serve hot with ice cream.

PUMPKIN PIE MUFFINS

SERVES 10 | PREP: 20–25 MINS, PLUS COOLING | BAKE: 25 MINS

There's no such thing as too much pumpkin during fall, so have a pumpkin muffin with a pumpkin drink like a Hot Pumpkin Pie (page 86) or a Boozy Pumpkin Spice Latte (page 40).

2¾ cups all-purpose flour
1½ cups rolled oats
1¼ teaspoons baking powder
¾ teaspoon baking soda
¼ teaspoon salt
2 teaspoons ground pumpkin pie spice (page 38)
½ cup brown sugar, firmly packed
½ cup granulated sugar
2 eggs
2 teaspoons vanilla extract
1 cup canned pumpkin puree
1½ tablespoons vegetable oil
1 cup milk of choice

1. Preheat the oven to 350°F. Line muffin pan with 10 muffin cups.
2. Put the flour, oats, baking powder, baking soda, salt, and pumpkin pie spice into a large bowl, and mix thoroughly to combine.
3. Beat the sugars, eggs, and vanilla extract in a mixing bowl, then add in the pumpkin puree, vegetable oil, and milk. Add the dry ingredients and beat until just mixed.
4. Divide the batter among the muffin cups. Bake in the preheated oven for 25 minutes until a toothpick inserted into the center of a muffin comes out clean.
5. Let the muffins rest in the pan for a few minutes until they are cool enough to handle, then transfer to a wire rack to cool completely.

PEAR & CARAMEL CRISP

SERVES 4 | PREP: 25-30 MINS | BAKE: 45-55 MINS

1 tablespoon unsalted butter, plus extra for greasing
4 large pears
¾ cup caramel sauce
ice cream, to serve

CRUMB TOPPING

1 cup all-purpose flour
1 teaspoon baking powder
1 stick unsalted butter, diced
⅔ cup brown sugar, lightly packed
2 tablespoons hazelnuts, chopped

1. Preheat the oven to 400°F. Lightly grease an 8x8-inch baking dish.

2. To make the crumb topping, put the flour and baking powder into a large mixing bowl, then use your fingertips to rub in the unsalted butter until crumbly. Stir in ¼ cup of the brown sugar and the chopped hazelnuts. Set aside.

3. Put the unsalted butter in a pan and melt over low heat. Meanwhile, peel, core, and coarsely chop the pears. Add pears to the pan and cook, stirring gently, for 3 minutes. Stir in the caramel and continue to cook, stirring, over low heat for another 3 minutes.

4. Transfer the pear-and-caramel mixture to the greased baking dish. Sprinkle the topping evenly over the top, then sprinkle the remaining sugar. Bake in the oven for 25–30 minutes the crumb topping is golden brown. Serve with ice cream.

INDEX